Meditation

A Comprehensive Guide To Meditation Practices And Techniques In Yoga And Vedanta

(Learn How To Declutter Your Mind And Reduce Anxious Thoughts By Practicing Mindful Thinking)

Judson Underwood

TABLE OF CONTENT

Introduction To Meditation 1

What Is Meditation 12

Stoic Methods: Good Or Evil? 60

A View Of The Future You Wish To Observe ...77

The First Exercise Is Breathing Through The Spine...114

Benefits Of Meditation 118

What Companions Want..123

Principal Advantages Of Mindful Breathing .128

Managing Unsettling Emotions 140

Introduction To Meditation

Despite its popularity, relatively few of us really comprehend what meditation entails. A regular occurrence is hearing meditators explain their practice incorrectly. In addition to the fact that many of us misunderstand meditation, yoga and meditation are often confused. I have also seen individuals who avoid meditation because they believe it would contradict with their religious beliefs. That is untrue. It highlights the misunderstandings and falsehoods about meditation that, in one way or another, prevent individuals from benefiting from it or from engaging in it.

Describe meditation.
A mind-training technique called meditation helps the mind acquire the abilities and power it needs to solve issues. In other words, meditation is a

solution to mental health issues. Similar to how there are several treatments for the various ailments a body might develop, there are numerous kinds of drugs, each of which is used to treat a particular mental health issue. Sufferings and stress are the two things that affect our minds the most often.

Relaxing the mind, being quiet, and doing nothing are all important aspects of meditation. It involves guiding the mind beyond regular conscious thought and into a relaxed, aware state. Contrary to popular belief, meditation does not involve focus, imagination, or surrendering control. True meditation is more than that; it is profound. It involves reaching a level of inner tranquility that can only be attained when the mind is quiet, at ease, yet very vigilant. All of this is geared at undergoing an inner metamorphosis that may assist us in reaching the highest state of consciousness and, eventually, our full human potential.

Despite the overlap, there is a connection between yoga and meditation. It's critical to recognize the terms' original context in order to comprehend how the two relate to one another. Yoga means unification in Sanskrit. The term "union" describes the relationship that exists between the soul (a person) and the Spirit (God or the universe). Yoga is thus the condition of "union" and a method of achieving the "state of union".

Deeply involved in yoga, the legendary eight limbs of yoga, which include meditation, were created by the ancient sage Patanjali. The eight limbs of yoga are, in no particular order, 1. Yama, which stands for the Do's, 2. The Don'ts are referred to as Nimaya. 3. Asanas that are positions-specific 4. Pranayama that addresses the Life Force or breath regulation, 5. The sense withdrawal term Pratyahara, 6. Concentration-related Dharana, 7. Dhyana, which means MEDITATION, and 8. Samadhi, which means reaching a state of spiritual bliss.

The meditation technique described in this book is intended to assist the mind in resolving its fundamental issues. This is helpful since we live in a volatile period and encounter problems every day that often depress us. We become worn out, stressed out, sad, and occasionally terror takes control. If we don't have any comfort, it becomes increasingly harder. For instance, when our friends turn on us, when our coworkers annoy us, and sometimes when our loved ones are absent when we need them most. Despite the fact that we need to be joyful at these moments, our mind weights itself down and causes mental discomfort. When we strive to comprehend the mind's workings, the mind begins to heal. Meditation helps us understand why the mind is going through that. Happier, more at peace with ourselves, and a deeper understanding of these circumstances are all results of mental health.

Working for true happiness—happiness that won't change and that we can always count on—is the key of meditation. Happiness requires work on our part to achieve. We are taught not to get complacent with fleeting joys. The wonderful part about meditation is that it helps you realize that happiness is something we all own and does not depend on anybody or anything else. You can experience pleasure via meditation without sacrificing the happiness of others, and you won't experience any harm or loss as a result.

When meditating, it is important to remember that the means by which the objective is attained are also beneficial. They are mental capacities and pursuits of which you are proud, at ease, and capable. We are advised to cultivate the qualities and characteristics of discernment, awareness, compassion, integrity, and honesty, which meditation fosters.

You will learn through the practice of meditation that contentment and pleasure come from within; you won't be stealing from anybody. The truth is that your happiness will never clash with that of another person. You have a central role in the process as the one who develops and cultivates your happiness. And you'll have more to share if you experience true joy from inside.

This illustrates why practicing compassion via meditation is not just about ourselves. Making it true that you cannot give better than you have, you will be in the ideal position to distribute happiness and love when you are really happy. And you become stronger after you get rid of your tension, concerns, and sorrows. As a result, you won't ever cause trouble for others around you. Because if you are weak and unable to resolve your problems, you will include others in your business rather than being the one to assist them when necessary.

Therefore, meditation teaches you the value of appreciating the things within of you that are deserving of it. That is, the need to be content, the need to be trustworthy, the need to be truly content, and how to achieve contentment by making an effort. You can overcome more than simply your daily mental issues with meditation. By strengthening your mind, you can cope with increasingly difficult life situations including trauma, disappointment, addiction, aging, disease, and the passing of loved ones. Because of this, the greatest way to sum up meditation is as "the way to total freedom while living at the moment."

Pick a song to pay close attention to. The song may be selected from your music library, or you can just turn on the radio and wait for a song to start playing.

Instead than focusing on the notes, beats, voice, or rhythm while listening to the music, pay attention to the spaces in between the sounds. Pay attention to the gaps in sound between notes, including stops and pauses. Keep an eye out for the song's stillness.

Have you ever considered how silence might prevent your favorite tunes from existing? Even if it only lasts for a millisecond, quiet is necessary for every note, rhythm, beat, and voice to emerge. There wouldn't be any noise without stillness, much alone music. This is not to imply that loudness and stillness are at odds; quite the contrary. Silence and sound go well together. So, did you hear the quiet that the music contained? Every time you hear music, keep practicing this. Watch for the moments of quiet that let the song continue.

Similar to this, we need quiet in order to allow life's rhythm to emerge. Unfortunately, a lot of people find it difficult to do this since our environment is imbalanced and values sound above stillness. Avoid midlife crisis noise, and don't be afraid of solitude. Silence is an effective treatment. Daily silent practice will help you discover fascinating new sounds and sights.

*Ten silent minutes of concentrated breathing. Say it out loud: "Be quiet. Listen. Keep quiet.

(Tell others about it with the hashtag #30DaysSilentSong)

Day 16

Exercise:

Spend 5-10 minutes dancing, music or not. If you are too nervous or ashamed to dance, keep in mind that you'll be alone yourself, so no one will be evaluating your incredible or appalling dancing abilities. You may do this exercise while sitting or in a meditative state by pacing your arm and hand movements to your preferred pace. There is no need for music.

Everyone agrees that dancing expresses happiness. Dancing is not only good for the body, but it's also great for the mind. When you dance, your mind experiences a magical, therapeutic change. While dancing with a partner or a group is lovely, dancing alone is fantastic. An enlightened state of being may be attained by a dancer who is alone, conscious of their body's feelings and movements, and completely present.

Life is like a dance." It flows, picks up pace, slows down, changes course, deviates from the beat, and has both a beginning and a finish. Consider your life as a dance while you're dancing; don't criticize it; just see it as a lovely dance, regardless of its pace and rhythm.

Silence for 15 minutes while breathing deliberately. Say it out loud: "Life is a dance, and I am always in rhythm."

(Share your story using the hashtag #30DaysDance.)

What Is Meditation

Meditation is a mental state in which you observe the entire flow of thoughts, feelings, emotions, and sensations through your five senses without becoming entangled in them. Maintaining body stillness. And merely observing what is occurring. - Beginners Level

Without knowledge, meditation is pointless. If you are enlightened and only then will you surrender your thoughts, you are in meditation; similarly, fire is hazardous and the earth is spherical. - Expert Level

Why do we need to meditate?

These thoughts would be useful if they were flowing in a particular direction or in a solution-oriented manner. However, this is not the case because our biology craves pleasure and avoids pain; it does not look for long-term solutions; and if something provides pleasure in the short term, the mind will focus on it. And avoid short-term discomfort, which will lead to a pleasant and comfortable existence in the long run. Because of our short-sightedness, we become addicted. If we can moderately control the delight, then it will be beneficial for both our biology and our lives. Thus, the delight cycle begins with comparison, wherein we find ourselves in a state of deficiency, and a desire to attain that which causes a state of unease and leads to a negative thought cycle. The mind is willing to pay any price to obtain delight and avoid suffering. These never-ending desires to acquire and amass possessions or to gratify oneself result in a negative thought cycle because the absence of the desired item is always accompanied by a disorder, a condition in which the mind is restless. Therefore, our biochemistry will always lead us to an agitated mind in this marketing-driven world where everyone vies for your attention in order to activate your pleasure cycle. Therefore, to live in this world, we require thoughts that lead to serenity, as a human caught in the pleasure cycle will always be in a cycle of overthinking, tension, melancholy, and other mental disorders. To see this structure in which we are ensnared, we must engage in meditation in which we can observe the entire movement and cease mind babble effortlessly. The purpose of meditation is to observe what is occurring within and without us. Meditation can only make your mind tranquil while you are meditating; afterwards, you will return to the cycle of overthinking. Therefore, one must understand the structure of the mind and discover a method to avoid overthinking and mental chatter. If you can remain mute for hours without speaking, then you have completed meditation.

As we've already heard, meditation is the practice of calming the mind by preventing peculiar thoughts. Am I correct?

Why did I choose indulgence?

As whatever your mind focuses on begins to expand, you become bound; however, if you are simply observing your thoughts, you are not ensnared. You become the object you are observing. In meditation, when you examine a thought, you will now view it as a consequence of something. You are distinct from your thinking.

Let us presume that you are neither your thoughts nor a thinker.

How can I assert that you do not think? Listen You are aware that you are living, correct? Clearly, everyone will affirm this. But pause, are things outside of you, such as the water in a river, living or nonliving? Clearly nonliving,

Here's the point. How can a body composed of nonliving material, elements, and matter be considered a living body? Our body is composed of 70 percent water, which is a nonliving substance. Furthermore, the intellect or brain is composed of matter. Can we say that our body is a robotic software that operates according to laws that science can measure? If so, what is the difference between a robot and our body? The difference is the knower, who experiences the presence of our various states. Without consciousness, the body cannot function, as in the case of coma patients whose bodies are alive but they are not. Here, consciousness is a material that sustains life, a material that is aware of both the presence and absence of thoughts; while awake, it is evident that someone is aware that thoughts, feelings, and sensations are projected onto it. But we also know the absence as in profound sleep, where there are no bodily sensations, except there we also know the absence of everything, which is a projection of conscious material.

Therefore, the thought or living entity can be described as the combination of consciousness and consciousness's content.

Consciousness content is continually activating and deactivating; it activates when we awaken.

The content of consciousness is deactivated when we are in a coma or profound slumber; in both cases, it is deactivated. Because of this, we do not experience our presence, but consciousness is still present and aware of everything's absence at that moment.

How does content of consciousness function?

Or

how our psyche functions?

Our mind operates on the presence of thought, which is activated by the brain's default configuration.

First, we must correct our misconceptions; in reality, everything is scientific. In actuality, our heartbeats are governed by a scientific principle. Numerous similar concepts include the sino atrial node, relaxation and compression, diastole or systole, and others. Where glucose is converted to energy, in the mitochondria, we inhale oxygen. So many objects operating in concert to maintain our system. And it is possible to monitor everything, and science is doing so effectively.

Stress, Anxiety, Meditation, And The Brain

Stress and apprehension both trigger the fight or flight response. But how are anxiety and tension related? Simply stated, stress is a condition of apprehension and dread that causes you to remain vigilant and prepare for impending hazards. This emotion is commonly referred to as the fight-or-flight response, which is designed to heighten your awareness and prepare you for potential hazards. However, prolonged exposure to this state can result in a variety of psychological and physical issues.

Due to the comparable negative effects they leave in their aftermath, it is simple to confuse stress with anxiety and anxiety with stress. However, while anxiety is primarily caused by elevated stress levels, tension can manifest in a variety of forms and be caused by a number of factors.

Stress can induce feelings of worry, sadness, anxiety, and anger, whereas anxiety only manifests as fear, trepidation, and dread. Numerous external factors, such as marital problems, financial crises, and emotional distress, can cause stress, whereas anxiety is an internal reaction to stress or neurological disorders.

How then do anxiety and tension affect the brain?

How Anxiety And Stress Affect The Brain

Several neurological studies indicate that chronic tension and anxiety can cause long-term changes in the brain's structure and function. The gray matter in your brain is known to be densely crammed with numerous nerve cell bodies and is primarily responsible for your brain's higher functions, including computation, thought, and decision-making.

Acute stress conditions and anxiety are known to reduce the quantity of gray matter in the brain, resulting in diminished cognitive function in highly stressed individuals. Even the hippocampus, the brain region responsible for governing essential brain functions such as emotions and memory, has been observed to decrease in size under acute stress conditions.

The amygdala is another sensitive region of the brain that stress and anxiety affect. The amygdala is a primitive brain structure located in the interior portion of the temporal lobe. Multiple subregions of the amygdala are responsible for essential brain functions such as learning, perception, emotion regulation, etc. According to studies, individuals exposed to high levels of stress have larger amygdala and more synaptic connections, and this increased amygdala size and connectivity is a significant cause of anxiety.

When stress and anxiety are not properly managed, they can alter the size and connectivity of the areas of the brain responsible for these cognitive functions, thereby causing a variety of psychological issues, such as distorted cognitive functions, irregular thought patterns, and decreased concentration.

How Meditation Influences The Brain

Multiple studies on meditators indicate that the hippocampus and frontal regions of the brain contain more gray matter as daily meditators age. These regions of the brain are in charge of response regulation and emotional regulation. This explains why meditating as a means of combating tension and anxiety helps you to fret less, become a more rational thinker, and achieve greater mental and emotional equilibrium.

In addition, research on individuals who practice daily meditation demonstrates a reduction in the neural connections and size of the amygdala. This reduces the visceral emotions that follow frightening situations, resulting in fewer anxiety issues.

After learning how stress and anxiety affect the brain and why meditation is an effective technique for coping with stress and anxiety, let's examine the steps necessary for effective meditation.

Fundamentals Of Successful Meditation

Follow the steps below to begin your meditation practice:

1.Choose a tranquil and comfortable environment

To maximize the effectiveness of your meditation, you must avoid as many distractions as feasible. A tranquil environment will enhance your concentration, allowing you to easily enter a deeper state of meditation.

Choose a location where you are less likely to experience auditory and visual distractions; this could be your residence, your office, or another location.

2.Select a suitable time

It is always advisable to set aside a specific time to meditate in order to cultivate the habit of daily meditation. Choose a time when you will have a few minutes of uninterrupted time and no distractions. Most individuals prefer to meditate in the morning because it is quieter and less hectic. Additionally, it establishes the tone for the day. However, if morning is not convenient for you, choose a time that is.

3.Dress accordingly

It may sound strange, but your attire can have a positive or negative effect on your meditation sessions. It is always recommended to wear unrestricted attire. Additionally, you should not be so heated that you want to sleep or so chilly that you are uncomfortable.

4.Do not overindulge

Your body is typically decomposing after a meal, so meditating immediately after eating may not be the best idea. Two hours after a supper is ideal. Additionally, you should not be too famished, as concentration would be impaired. In such circumstances, it is best to consume a moderate refreshment and then meditate.

5.Choose a convenient posture.

Just as essential as meditating is assuming the proper seated or standing position, as distress will prevent you from concentrating on meditating. Below are meditation-friendly positions.

6. Learn to focus on your breathing

You must learn to tune into your body's sensations as a beginner. Your respiration is your most reliable anchor in every moment. In order to reduce tension, overcome anxiety, and feel great, you must master the art of focusing on your breath and becoming familiar with all the emotions and sensations your breath elicits during meditation.

7. Experiment with various methods

Numerous meditation techniques exist for combating tension and anxiety. It is essential that you determine which one is best for you and focus on that. To determine which one works best for you, you may need to experiment with various methods and techniques. The meditation technique that provides you with the most tension and anxiety alleviation should become your daily preference.

The next chapter will discuss various meditation techniques that you can attempt.

Mindfulness Practice

This is without a doubt the simplest and most prevalent meditation technique, and it is quite effective at reducing tension and anxiety. This method is actually quite straightforward. Here are the methods for practicing attentive meditation:

1. By now, I'm assuming you've selected a peaceful location and time for your meditation session.

2. Determine the length of your meditation and time it using a timer. A chronograph can be useful. Beginners

should limit their duration to five to ten minutes. You can gradually extend your meditation sessions until you can meditate for 45 to 60 minutes. Depending on your daily timetable, you can meditate once or twice daily.

3.Sit comfortably: You can experiment with various seating positions to determine which one makes you feel the most relaxed. You may choose to lie on a bed, cushion, meditation mat, chair, bed, and so on. No matter what you're sitting on, sit upright and avoid perching or slouching. Ensure that your upper limbs are parallel to your upper body. Permit the wrists to settle on the legs.

4.Lower your jawline slightly and permit your gaze to fall forward. You may lower your eyelids slightly. You can close your eyes to block out visual distractions, but you may not need to if you can meditate with your eyes open without focusing on what you see.

5.Spend some moments being present. Try to unwind. Focus your full awareness on your respiration and the sensations it creates in your body.

6.Follow and experience each of your breaths. Pay close attention to the air passing through your mouth and nose, as well as the rising and falling of your thorax and midsection. Focus on one of the areas that your respiration affects and the sensations they produce.

7.When meditating, learn not to engage the concepts that cross your consciousness. During meditation, your mind will occasionally wander; this is normal. It is essential to acknowledge the thoughts without reacting, engaging, grappling, or evaluating them. Simply sit, pay attention, recognize the thought, and return your focus to your breathing.

8.When the timer beeps, raise your gaze, open your eyes if they are closed, and take a few seconds to observe your immediate surroundings. Observe any intriguing images and noises in the environment. Take note of how your body feels after meditating mindfully.

Observe your thought and emotion patterns. Consider your plans for the remainder of the day and take a moment to reflect.

There is nothing else to attentive meditation. The more you practice mindful meditation, the more the portions of your brain that have been altered by anxiety and stress regain their normal structure, connectivity, and functionality, allowing you to fret less, feel less overwhelmed, and live blissfully ever after.

Although practicing mindful meditation at specific times of the day is beneficial, it may not be as effective as incorporating mindfulness into your daily routine. How can you incorporate mindfulness into your daily life?

Observant Shower

If you've ever felt immersed in the moment while singing in the shower, you'll understand the enchanting effect this can have.

As the water flows down your epidermis to remove physical grime, you can envision all of your tension and concerns being removed. Consider how the water caresses your epidermis. Imagine the tension and anxiety in your mind evaporating with the water vapor and being rinsed away with the soil. Focus on the sensation of air moving in and out of your nostrils as you breathe evenly.

Utilizing your preferred essential oil will enhance the tranquil effect of this contemplative bath. Some essential oils, such as lavender, are renowned for their remarkable soothing effects.

When you are finished with your shower, be grateful and carry this gratitude and mindfulness into the rest of your day's activities.

Conscious Eating

When it comes to your health and wellbeing, there is more to consider than what you consume. How you prepare your food and how you consume it are crucial factors. Mindful dining improves health because it engages all five senses. Here is how to incorporate meditation into your mealtimes:

•Before eating, express gratitude that you have sustenance and the ability to consume.

Before consuming, take the time to appreciate the appearance and aroma of your food, as well as its nutritional value.

•Take a portion, place the utensil or spoon down, and ruminate for as long as possible to enable the flavors to permeate your taste receptors before swallowing. You can count the number of times you chew mentally.

Take Mindful Walks

According to research findings, walking mindfully can be an effective method to reduce stress and anxiety. Those who are too anxious to engage in other forms of physical activity should engage in mindful strolling. This is a wonderful option because you can take short breaks throughout the day to engage in it for a few minutes. Adding mindfulness to a walk provides additional benefits, including a calm mind and nerves, enhanced concentration and focus, and a greater sense of well-being. Here are the steps:

- Determine the starting point and duration of your daily mindful walk. Ideal is a natural setting such as a garden or forest trail.

- While doing so, you can listen to your beloved tune through your headphones.

- As with all other meditation techniques, begin by concentrating on your breathing.

- Be aware of your surroundings as you walk around. Observe the flora when walking through a garden, field, or forest trail. Observe the aromas. Appreciate the variety of the flowers' gorgeous hues. If possible, touch some and observe how they feel.

- Enjoy the moment and let go of all domestic and professional concerns.

Feel the calm and serenity in your heart as you live in the present moment.

• When you are finished, be appreciative of the natural splendor that surrounds you. Be thankful for the unrestricted air you breathe and the freedom to move around.

My Awakening

With a laceration above my brow (blood dripping like cherry pie filling down my face) and upper teeth shattered and a fractured cranium, I was struck out cold when the local paramedics and police pulled me off the pavement one sweltering night in southern Mississippi, a stone's throw from the Gulf Coast.

Everclear was the lethal agent.

Imagine grain alcohol oozing out of your pores. Consider someone who, upon awakening, is slurring, staggering, and struggling not to fall on their face. Imagine a Midwestern "Yankee" reporter plummeting from a series of newsrooms in the north to a grimy crime scene in a ghetto where an ill-fated scheme to finance an escalating drug habit went horrifically wrong.

Imagine an unplanned, lengthy vacation in the Deep South. Imagine the old chain gangs in the humid humidity of the marsh. Imagine photographs of yellow crime scene tape and red and blue glaring lights on damp, dark pavement. Imagine an enraged throng seeking so-called "street justice" with deep southern dialects — southern drawl combined with southern street vernacular — and people dispersed about while police officers maintained a solid barrier between me and the crowd. The paramedics patched me up swiftly before rushing me to the emergency room. Moments later, I am treated in a hospital that is ten years behind the times. Imagine doctors in the wilderness using pagers. Consider the futility of it all. Consider the cultural upheaval.

Outside my door, a voice stated, "Yes, there is no reason to keep him here overnight." I presumed the doctor was speaking with the authorities. I was handcuffed to a hospital gurney with an officer standing sentry in front of me.

Consider startling news. Imagine more photographs, but with my visage in them and my name in the captions. I had become front-page news. Within a few months of using heavy narcotics — I was swept up on the Gulf Coast (years after Hurricane Katrina) — I lost my journalism career in an instant.

"Tonight's top news story: a northern man delivered a dose of 'street justice'."

Imagine mugshots rather than photographs. It was the top story that day in 2009 in that region of the state and the nation because, as in any newsroom, the maxim "if it bleeds, it leads" determined a story's importance. My registration photo at the jail depicted a visage so bruised and swelling that they were compelled to display it to their audience.

A few days later, as we all watched from a detention compartment just south of Hattiesburg, the reporter stated, "Wrong neighborhood." "Wrong time."

After being transported from the hospital, hours later I was lying in a holding cell nude and frigid without a blanket or pillow while on suicide watch and detoxification. Suicide inmates were provided with "smock" suits, which was all I had. Imagine more photographs. Imagine fresh blood on a frigid, unyielding prison floor.

An officer yelled, "Hey Yankee, if you don't get your head off the floor, you're going to catch something that will rot a hole in your face!" Despite his laughter, he was not teasing. In less than a week, a staph infection appeared on my thigh; it was a marble-sized lesion filled with greenish-yellow fluid. Some of the other detainees advised me to conceal it from the officers lest I be placed in seclusion. In any event, the medical facility was essentially "the hole."

Imagine more somber photographs.

A thousand miles separated me from home. It was my first time being incarcerated. Before a few weeks, I had an important desk and position at an important Ohio newspaper. I believed I was a significant individual. People praised my writing style, despite the fact that I had been consistently intoxicated at work for over a year. In the past, it was speculated that I was destined for New York Times prominence. However, they were incorrect. One can only go on for so long in the manner in which I had been going, pursuing anything and everything that altered how I felt, enslaved by my extremely egotistical desires, and casually committing new offenses with the passage of each excruciating day to fund my addiction.

The Ohio State University awarded me a bachelor's degree in Journalism, which I displayed on my wall. I had received a variety of awards over the years. Consider civilian commendations extended by law enforcement. Consider honor roll mentions. Consider reporting honors. Thousands of my articles and photographs were published in newspapers and periodicals across the globe over the course of ten years. I have appeared as a guest on national television, including Nancy Grace and A&E, as well as a number of local stations, for various reasons.

Initially, I convinced myself that I required alcohol to compose. Never in a million years did I imagine it would place me on the wrong side of a detention cell, let alone hundreds of miles away from home and screwed up in numerous ways.

How did this come about? I queried myself. I was in a million places at once, my mind rushing back 10 years to recall my path and forward 10 years to the prison sentence I faced as a result. My thoughts were in a frenzy. An impenetrable veil descended upon me. The current situation was simply too much. And there was no place to hide and nothing to dull the agony. Add this palpable terror to my excruciating head injuries, the pain of the opioid and alcohol withdrawals, and the hunger pangs from the standard prison deprivation diet, and I had never before endured such suffering. It was a trinity of physical, mental, and spiritual despondency.

"I come from a good family," I told the detectives who interrogated me about the incident. The judge denied my parole because I was from Ohio and I was charged with burglary. According to them, I posed a flight risk. Perhaps they were correct.

"I've never been in trouble," I implored. "I have a substance problem. I need assistance."

They chuckled and stated, "You all have drug issues." You all require assistance."

Imagine a frigid steel door slamming so violently that the echoes are still audible today. When I first started down this path many years ago, I vowed I'd never cross certain lines — too many lines to count — but now that I'm gazing back, they're all a horrifyingly long haze. Whenever I consider my substance addiction, I frequently recall the day I became a professional writer. I recall thinking, "Perhaps I ought to stop all this partying now that I'm earning more than my peers and am on par with the editor of 10 years." At the age of 20, I was an English major at Oregon State University with wild-eyed confidence that I would one day write a great American novel that would transform the world. In 2001, when I was recruited by my community newspaper, I altered my concentration to journalism. Although I abandoned that ambition, I knew in my heart that I would one day write a best-seller. Without a shadow of a doubt, I've always felt that this was my purpose on earth. I believed, however, that a reporter's salary would cover my expenses at the time. And it would be enjoyable! And it was all tremendously enjoyable.

What about alcohol? Certainly, it helped me write initially. It brought out a creative, fearless aspect of me that could speak with authority on any topic, regardless of whether I sounded like an imbecile. It felt nice. In addition, I believed that every writer drank. All the excellent ones, at the very least. During my first year as a reporter, I struck the ground running, but alcohol began to confound me. I simply could not stop, and the more I tried, the more difficult it became. Today, a wise old Indian proverb comes to mind: "First, the man drinks. The beverage then drinks. Then alcohol consumes the man." Today, I recognize that the adage "what you resist will persist" is accurate. I had to learn through my own actions that the most dangerous type of person is one who has lost control of his or her desires, pursuing them blindly through the night amidst a field of hidden explosives. Additionally, the most deadly sort of individual is one who is terrified of his own shadow. Imagine being in a self-imposed prison — a purgatory that continued to spin me faster and faster in tumultuous circles while I descended into complete and utter lunacy.

During this period of my existence, each 24-hour period was a vicious, unstoppable cycle, a roller-coaster voyage through some kind of modern madhouse. I would hurry out the door each morning with an enormous, nearly paralyzing hungover to get to work late and assemble the latest breaking news from local police agencies, the municipal police department, the sheriff's office, or both. I would swear not to repeat the previous night's actions, condemning myself. All morning long, I would consume copious amounts of coffee and vow to God that I would stop. My only wholesome fixation was going to the gym at lunchtime, when I felt marginally better. After a good workout, healthy stretch, and sweating the dirt out of my pores, I would shower, complete my workday, and then spend the evening alone in my own apartment as a single bachelor. Facing tedium, I attempted to exercise self-control by limiting myself to "just one," which never worked. One developed into two. Two increased to three. Three turned into... repeating the entire cycle only to awaken slightly more perplexed the next day. On occasion, I would ponder if I had died and gone to purgatory when I awoke in the morning. Literally. As a child, I was fascinated by science fiction and horror films and had read innumerable novels. Stephen King and Shakespeare were my favourite authors.

Some mornings, this concept of being in purgatory was very real.Have I perished and entered hell?I'd question myself. One of the most terrifying aspects of this purgatory was that no one could recall entering it. One simply awakens there. One suffers tremendously in this inferno, but one never completely realizes they are in hell; one would not venture to do so because doing so would cause even greater suffering by making their stay permanent... If this was purgatory, I reasoned, the devil's greatest ploy was "euphoric recall," this deceptive radiance of attraction that surrounds our desires. It is a deception of the mind for something that has repeatedly caused so much suffering to appear alluring for a moment. What is the opposite of divine intervention? Countless times, I unsuccessfully attempted to outwit my alcoholism. My alcoholism always remained two steps ahead of me. Working at the county fair for the local newspaper, I had no idea that one day I would discover a solution to this imbibing disaster. The week of the county fair was nightmare week for this rural publication. Consider over time. Consider searing weather, 16-hour workdays, and the presence of livestock, carnival attractions, and cattle.

I was photographing and writing about what appeared to be every goat, sheep, poultry, pig, cattle, and other 4-H-friendly family farm animals. Consider pie competitions without press samples. This includes award-winning textiles, photographs, essays, chili recipes, etc.

We are discussing horse races and demolition derbies, noxious fair cuisine from so-called "carnies," and there I was, a worn-out, despondent reporter in his early 20s with circles under his eyes like luggage, struggling to keep it all together. I will never forget that day because a photographer who worked with me gave me a gift — the first one is always free but comes at a high price — that altered the trajectory of my life radically.

"It's OxyContin," he declared. "Eat it, and it will cure your hangover." He chuckled. And I requested two.

He initially hesitated, but ultimately consented to give two. I chewed on them rather naively. Having never taken an opioid before, I did not know what to anticipate. However, they hit me rather quickly and did a great deal more than alleviate my nausea. That evening, I walked on clouds and for one night felt like a god. It was such a profound impression that it still gives me shivers. What is contrary to divine intervention?

This substance gave me boundless energy and a level of euphoria that altered my life immediately. It was the first time in my adult life that I forgot about alcohol. Opioid euphoria is frequently compared to witnessing a magnificent dragon that one could almost claim as one's own. This is the mysterious dragon I would pursue at any cost. It was as if I had a new God, because I no longer had a hangover. After overcoming alcoholism, I developed a new addiction. Consider turning on the light switch in a dark room. Imagine a blindingly bright white light.So, this is the answer I've been looking for?I believed that this material was made for me, or that I was made for it. What is contrary to divine intervention? Christian upbringing was how I was raised. We were frequently asked as infants, "What would Jesus do?"

In my twenties, I rephrased this question as "What would NOT Jesus do?"

Normal individuals would anticipate that this calamity in Mississippi would be my lowest point, and in many respects, they were correct. Nevertheless, it was not the end. The journey to rock bottom consisted of a series of steppingstones strewn along the pitch-black valley of death, where friends and acquaintances frequently fell by the wayside. I eventually developed a simple prayer to help me endure these agonizing and dismal times: "Yes, though I walk through the valley of the shadow of death, I will not fear evil. Because I am the nastiest @#$% in the valley." By the time I was in my mid- to late-20s, I was a trim, 250-pound weightlifting juggernaut.

I would ask myself, "How did I get here?" whenever I had a moment of clarity. "How long have I lived in this darkness?" The even more important query was, "How am I still alive?" Too many times to count, I should have died or should not have been miraculously resurrected from the dead.

Consider memories.

Consider a child from the Midwest who was raised in a typical Christian family. We were an example of a "nuclear family." I never envisaged as a child growing up in a small Ohio town that I would become an alcoholic or an addict — a pitiful captive to my egotistical desires who repeatedly caused damage to the people I loved. Who however? No infant desires to become an alcoholic or substance addict. No one ever imagines they will use waste water to fire up or have to slumber in the forests during the coldest months of the year in Ohio. No one believes they would be involved in more than a dozen car accidents over the course of ten years, or that a single injection of Narcan would revive their lifeless body. No one dares. In my earliest memories of growing up in a middle-class family with two younger siblings, we labored financially as my father fought his own afflictions, perhaps passed down like a family heirloom. I recall rummaging in dumpsters, using gasoline to remove head lice from our neighbors' hair, and scrounging for spare change. Before my two siblings were old enough to remember the difficult times, my mother completed nursing school and my father settled into his role as a parent.

Nonetheless, my childhood ambition was to become an actor, but more significantly, a writer and storyteller. Years later, when I entered college with a palpable sense of optimism, I was met with early success. I obtained my ideal job as a writer, and for years I worked diligently in the public view while, behind the scenes, my battle with alcohol morphed into a living horror from which I could only find respite by substituting other substances for alcohol. Soon, in the midst of my burgeoning, promising career, my "secret struggle" became extremely public through a succession of humiliations and low points I never imagined were humanly possible. If someone asked me to describe the living hell I endured for more than 15 years, I could paint a vivid picture of a tornado's path of destruction that cost me my dignity, career, and a small fortune. And, like a tornado, it wreaked havoc on the lives of so many decent people in its course.

As they say in AA, "the ends are always the same: jails, institutions, and death." I've visited all of them, including emergency rooms, rehabilitation centers, and prisons. I have overdosed multiple times. I have defied mortality numerous times. And when you combine all this insanity in my personal life with the atrocities, fatalities, homicides, crime, and suffering I witnessed as a crime reporter for a decade, it's no surprise that my nightmares were filled with horrific imagery. I had a vast array of supernatural encounters at a young age, which was either a blessing or a burden. I attempted to drown out all of this for years. It is a true miracle that I slept at all. The irony of fate lies in the fact that I eventually became the very things I wrote about. Imagine criminals. Consider the term felon. Think narcotics supplier. Consider the hypocrisy. Consider your consequences.

As with most things let unrestrained in the darkness, these creatures eventually emerged into the light, and what a hideous spectacle it was. I recall making a narcotic transaction with a man one evening, and then covering his arrest the following week. Photos on the front page, my byline below the headline, and my alleged co-author being arrested.

Snapshots.

Before going on national television, I remember taking narcotics on the back of a commode in a studio. "Five Killed in Memorial Day Massacre" was the headline. In addition, I recall seeing and hearing things that most people would not venture to discuss in public. I have witnessed incomparable horrors. And yet, I have forgotten an incalculable number of things. These are merely "snapshots" because I did not withstand torment to be able to relate combat experiences. Certain awakenings are more painful than others. However, this is a narrative of redemption and hope. I only depict the atrocities of my past so that others who may be bound in a similar darkness can see that there is hope. A spiritual awakening through the power of consciousness represents this glimmer of hope. Anyone can do it. And I am not solely referring to "recovering" in the sense of collecting coinage at meetings and living a mundane existence. I am here to tell you that you can use your pain, your suffering, as a tool and a motivator to raise your level of consciousness and transcend merely "recovering" to thriving, to living an abundant life filled with joy, health, wealth, and prosperity, with inner and outer rewards beyond your wildest aspirations. I am an example of this. I used to claim that I was a maestro of self-destruction. My masterwork is the resurrection of the dead. My nervous system has been rewired, and my existence is now a voyage of self-realization. My life has been a completely delightful, rewarding roller coaster ride that I am fortunate to be able to share with others, despite the most excruciating agony and suffering. Because I have discovered the Secret Power of Consciousness, I am inspired to be alive each and every morning, and there is no turning back! I have rebuilt my life and am once again writing, as I believe the creator summoned me to do.

Having discarded all of that, I'd like to believe that my narrative of redemption began in 2012, when I learned I was going to be a father and began attending Alcoholics Anonymous meetings. At the time, I did what was right for my daughter and took a step back to assess my life, which was shattered into a million fragments. If there's one thing I've done well over the past decade — in and out of recovery rooms multiple times — it's my persistence in returning, failure after failure, and refusal to give up despite the persistent appearance of hopelessness. Each time I amassed a period of time in recovery, whether it was a few months or a year, I discovered something incredibly valuable. My most recent performance, which concluded in 2017, was unquestionably among the most ignominious and degrading of all. In 2016, following a lengthy period of recovery and life reconstruction, I relapsed. This resulted in a journey to jail. After my release from prison, I became destitute in my birthplace, where no one would take me in, and I was forced to sleep in the forests in hazardous conditions. First time alone in the wilderness, I discovered a tiny cabin to overnight in. And I tried my hardest to remain toasty.

Something occurred in my heart while I was in those woods and along the railroad tracks back home, causing me to cry for the first time in years. I broke down and realized who I was and what I had become. Here I was again, approaching 40 years of age, replicating the same errors I had been repeating for years. Out there in the bitter cold, confined in this excruciating spiritual darkness, I was famished and devastated, with no money, no place to go, and no one to speak with. I was totally sober and devoid of all human amenities and decency. As I settled into this small cabin, which had as much floor space as a small closet or coffin, alone with my transient thoughts one night, a sense of peace and serenity came over me, and time seemed to stand still. That night, I nearly died from hypothermia. That evening, everyone's mobile phone received a freeze advisory alerting them to bring their canines inside because temperatures were plummeting perilously below zero. Because I had nowhere else to go, I slept in the frigid cold outside. When I awoke the next morning, everything around me was frozen solid, and I felt a severe agony radiating all the way down to my bones.

I was entirely sober and amazed that I had survived the night without freezing to death. I began to realize how many near calls I had throughout my life, and for the first time, I was astonished that I was still alive. Then an event occurred. In the serenity of this dark, early dawn, it was as if someone had struck a match, igniting a supernova of insight and comprehension — a moment of clarity and recollection from the depths of my being. I felt instantly as ancient as the constellations. I perceived I had been caught in a dream that had devolved into a nightmare, running in place endlessly and achieving nothing.

All of reality collapsed in a split second, in an unbounded instant. It felt as if I had been struck by lightning, as if the heavens had parted and revealed the entirety of existence as an interminable river of consciousness, ever-flowing deep and broad. I then recognized that death was an illusion. There is no conventional mortality. Looking at my addictions and my path up to this point, it was as if the universe were saying, "There is no escape. You must proceed."

Behind an infinite number of forms, it appeared so precisely and excruciatingly evident, was a single infinite consciousness. It was as if I had amnesia and for a split second I remembered everything. But I wasn't alone. It appeared as if humanity, a species with amnesia, had been repeating the same mistakes over and over again for an unfathomably long time, enslaving, killing, and exalting ourselves as we all marched forward in this vast cosmic dance with no end — churning in cycle after cycle amid season after season. It was as if my mind and this infinite mind merged for a split second, but in that split second, I saw EVERYTHING. It appeared that I knew EVERYTHING. I still recall how that moment altered my life and set me on a path of happiness and service to others.

Stoic Methods: Good Or Evil?

There are numerous streams of thought in the globe, ranging from commerce to philosophy. Some institutions have gained greater popularity than others, while others are still in their infancy. Different institutions emphasis various emphases. However, not all institutions adhere to best practices. What are best practices, and how can they be utilized to your advantage?

Plato founded one of the earliest streams of thought in philosophy, Platonism. It spread through his 300-year-old Platonic Academy, which was devoted to the pursuit of knowledge and truth via philosophical discourse. Aristotle is the most well-known student of Platonism; he went on to write some of the most influential books in contemporary philosophy, such as There is also Existentialism, the goal of which is not necessarily absolute truth but rather the search for meaning within oneself despite any objective reality outside oneself. Stoicism is the subject of this book, which contends that humans should learn to surmount dread and suffering by embracing them with dignity rather than attempting to flee from or fight against them. Nevertheless, there can be no definitive moral authority on what life means to humans, as we all have different perspectives based on our individual experiences.

However, how can you differentiate between a good and a poor practice?

Oftentimes, individuals wander erratically in search of pleasure and fulfillment, but fail to do so. This is because people have neglected the fundamental principles of Stoicism, an ancient philosophy that teaches us how to live well despite lacking "things." A skilled Stoic understands how to make the most of any circumstance; regardless of the situation, they have a firm grip on their emotions. A competent Stoic can learn to be content with what they have because they believe their desires and requirements will be met when the time is right.

Common Errors You Might Make

Stoic misunderstandings are quite natural and prevalent. A common misconception regarding Stoics is that they are dispassionate. Stoics believe in experiencing emotions but not responding to them. Another misconception is that Stoics do not speak or interact with others, whereas in reality they can be quite gregarious! There is more to stoicism than always appearing to be in profound thought while reclining still.

This ancient philosophy emphasizes wisdom and harmony with the natural world. Even though it lacks dogmatic premises, it can teach you valuable life lessons if properly practiced. This book discusses essential Stoic concepts, such as The Four Pillars and how to honor the virtuous life.

Understanding and respecting the virtues makes it simpler to avoid common errors made by individuals who are new to Stoicism. It is a pragmatic philosophy that is significantly simpler to implement than it sounds. There are seemingly limitless methods to apply the theory, but many people are still perplexed and discouraged by it because they make errors in practice. However, it is perfectly acceptable for even the most experienced individual to succumb to their emotions on occasion. Getting out of a bad circumstance is one of the most important Stoic principles. This beginner's guide aims to clarify common misconceptions and eliminate obstacles preventing modern people from utilizing this ancient and potent wisdom.

It is common for people to misunderstand the Stoic philosophy, and as a result, they frequently do not adhere to its requirements.

The most common errors when practicing this philosophy are suppressing emotions, sacrificing pleasure, and using it as an excuse to harm others. Being a better person is essential; harming others for one's own benefit is not acceptable according to this philosophical teaching.

People who practice Stoicism in the present day and age do not consider their emotions when evaluating a situation. One of the tenets of Stoic philosophy is to maintain ataraxia, which means "peacefulness" or "tranquility." This aspect derives from a conception of virtue as a form of interior fortitude. It is about confronting adversity without dread or resentment, instead resigning oneself to facing the adversity head-on with courage and dignity. Epictetus asked, "What are your aspirations? To have things carried out in accordance with your desires? Therefore, do so! Gain command of yourself![VM7]"

Create an Internal Control Point

Do you feel controlled by external forces? Do you appear to have little or no control over your life's events? Consider what it would be like if you could influence the outcome of any given situation at any time.

Everyone should learn more about control locus. The underlying concepts are empirical and straightforward to study; they are applicable in clinical settings, classrooms, and families. [VM8]

This concept elaborates on the extent to which a person believes they are in charge of their own existence. In 1954, Julian Rotter coined the term. Personal, Chance, Powerful Others, Society or Social Institutions, Uncontrollable or Ill-Fated Events (sometimes termed Learned Helplessness), and Mystical Forces are the six distinct loci of control he created.

The locus of control reveals the extent to which an individual believes they have control over their own existence. Rotter frequently used it to explain why some cultures appear to be more prone to externalizing their problems, such as blaming the government or others, rather than accepting personal responsibility. It is also believed to contribute to specific personality disorders such as paranoia and narcissism.

The locus of control is frequently described as 'internal' or 'external.' An external locus of control is the belief that external forces determine your actions, whereas an internal locus of control is the belief that your actions are your own responsibility.

Stoicism has taught individuals how to cultivate an internal locus of control for centuries. This philosophy utilizes ancient wisdom from thousands of years ago to assist those who find this concept implausible. Internal locus training can help you focus on your objectives and feel more confident about yourself.

Negative Visualization

Practicing Stoic disciplines such as negative visualization (imagining your worst fears coming true) and voluntary discomfort (doing something unpleasant) teaches us not to fear events that are genuinely improbable or even improbable. Reducing our apprehension of these occurrences permits us to make more rational decisions.

The Stoic philosophy of living in harmony with nature, despite not always having absolute control over our external circumstances, was an early systematic human psychology that provided a distinctive lens through which to view life's challenges. Stoicism is advantageous for sustaining emotional stability, which is sufficient for the majority of individuals who fear they are following an extremist path. Even fewer people use it as more than a coping mechanism or a 'philosophy of life' these days.

This exercise can also help individuals identify their weaknesses, such as when they cannot come up with a solution to a hypothetically negative situation, so that they are aware of the areas in which they need to develop. It has been demonstrated that employing this type of thinking can make people happier because it reduces their anxiety about things going awry because they have considered how to manage the situation and dealt with some of their emotions about it.

To exercise this as you go about your day, take a moment to consider the possibility that you could lose all of your material possessions. Imagine what your life would be like if you lost everything today, tomorrow, or next week. You could also consider the possibility that a loved one could pass away at any moment, as this is equally probable.

This strategy is founded on advice given by Epictetus in Discourses 3-4 and reiterated in Letter 10.

Every morning, Marcus Aurelius, the Stoic Emperor of Rome, said to himself, "You have control over your consciousness, not external occurrences. This realization will provide you with fortitude. This uplifting affirmation encapsulates what it means to be a Stoic; we control how we respond to situations, even if they are unavoidable. There is still a degree of discretion in how we respond to them. This exercise is designed to help you become more receptive of negative outcomes and embrace them with grace.

Ideologies, Beliefs, & Principles

Stoics put their beliefs into practice through judgment. They believed that someone with "moral and intellectual perfection" would not experience emotional disturbances. This psychological training was crucial to Stoic practice; as Musonius Rufus put it, "the aim of philosophy is to live in accordance with or harmony with nature.... We will attain this objective if we consider accurately about divine and human matters." Philosophy need not be monotonous, tiresome, or challenging. Philosophy is a method of life that can transform one's beliefs and actions for the better. You can accomplish this transformation by meditating on the words of renowned philosophers, such as Seneca, Marcus Aurelius, and Epictetus, among others.[VM9]

The Stoic philosophy is thousands of years old. It seeks to help you embrace a peaceful, joyful existence and realize your full potential by teaching you how to use reason to control the perils that threaten humanity. The Stoics divided their philosophy into three components: logic, physics, and ethics.

They believed that to live a fulfilling life, one must acknowledge that all humans are subject to a predetermined fate or destiny. In contrast to Plato's view that reason is more important than emotion (known as Platonism), the Stoics believed that humans could live rationally by training themselves to control their emotions over time.

Stoicism's central tenets are as follows:

Resistance to intense emotions

disregard for mortality

Taciturnity

Self-sufficiency

The ideology of stoicism may foster an internal resistance to objective requirements (Ladouceur et al., 2008). It can yield positive results when applied to psychosocial aspects of healthcare settings, such as communication with health professionals and bearing with terminal illness.

Sometimes, the four Stoic virtues are referred to as the cardinal virtues:

Practical intelligence (prudence)

Moderation (temperance)

Courage (fortitude)

Honesty (justice)

However, none of them are considered virtues on their own. They may be viewed as characteristics or dispositions that strengthen and elevate humanity, but they must be utilized in tandem so that one does not overpower the others.

The Stoics pursued moral concepts and enduring principles. They formulated eight principles that serve as the basis for living a decent existence [VM10]. These principles have been utilized by individuals from all aspects of life and can assist you in reaching your objectives.

The world is rational.

Illness, destitution, and death are natural and not evil.

Living in accordance with rational nature is virtuous.

Apathy is irrational (passion).

Wisdom is the foundation of every virtue.

The universe is ruled by a rational law.

There is nothing positive or evil about pleasure.

Virtue should be pursued out of duty, not out of desire.

The focus of stoic philosophy is on how to live well, not simply exist. It is about being content with what you have and making the most of it, as opposed to desiring more or wishing things were different. Through it, you will learn to make better decisions in your daily life by using logic rather than emotion. This philosophy will lead to increased satisfaction and fulfillment, as well as enhanced interpersonal relationships.

Major Figures

This section provides a concise introduction to two of Stoicism's most influential figures.

Marcus Aurelius

Marcus Aurelius, a key figure in Stoicism, was a philosopher who lived in a chaotic and violent time. From 154 to 161 CE, he fought against the invading Germanic tribes. Marcus Aurelius was an Emperor of Rome. He was born around 121 CE and died around 180 CE during the 2nd century CE. As a member of the Antonine dynasty, he ruled. He was the last of the emperors collectively known as the 'Five Good Emperors,' who ruled during the period when the Roman Empire attained its greatest extent.

He was also widely known for his contributions to Stoic philosophy. Meditations is considered by some to be one of the finest philosophical compositions ever composed. This well-known Stoic text is a resource for self-improvement. It contains Marcus Aurelius' personal thoughts on Stoic philosophy. This historical work has become one of the most widely read philosophical texts ever composed and has had a lasting impact on Western popular culture.

In addition, he became a renowned polymath, leading a type of research institute, composing poetry, constructing a vast canal system, and even conducting meteorological observations. Marcus was, however, best known as a conqueror; he expanded Roman imperial authority further than any previous emperor, eventually reigning over the entire Mediterranean region.

Zeno of Caesarea

Zeno of [VM11]Citium was an additional notable Stoic philosopher. Some consider him the 'parent' of the Stoic school of philosophy, which he taught in Athens beginning around 300 B.C. Based on the moral concepts of the Cynics, Zeno developed Stoicism with a strong emphasis on righteousness and the mental tranquility that comes from living a life of virtue in accordance with nature.

Circa 334 BCE, or possibly 336 or 324 BCE, he was born in Citium, Cyprus (though this is debatable). His early existence is virtually unknown, as he tells us nothing about himself. He was the first instructor of Stoicism, and the philosophy derives its name from the location where he taught. It derives from the Greek word stoa, which means "porch or colonnade" or "passageway," a structure where people congregated to discuss life, morality, philosophy, politics, and other fundamental topics.

His Dichotomy paradoxes are a set of specific paradoxical arguments that purport to demonstrate that motion is impossible or that change is an illusion. Among the variations is the Arrow (or Achilles), which demonstrates the impossibility of motion, and others. Over time, numerous variants arose, with their proponents presenting challenging counterarguments.

This apparent paradox's contradictory reasoning has been known since antiquity, but it was only formalized as a part of classical logic in the modern era, including the refutations that followed.

A View Of The Future You Wish To Observe

Creating a compelling vision of the life you desire may appear to be a frivolous and fanciful waste of time, but it is actually one of the most effective strategies for attaining the life you desire. Creating a life vision may appear to be a frivolous and fanciful waste of time, but it is not. Consider the concept of a life vision as a compass that guides you toward the best courses of action and decisions that will bring you closer to experiencing the life of your dreams. This is possibly the most useful method to consider the concept of a life vision.

Why You Obligatorily Need a Vision

Experts and real-world success tales lend credence to the notion that having a clear vision for the future significantly improves your odds of achieving success compared to what you would be able to achieve without a vision. Consider the process of creating your life vision as the creation of a road map for achieving your personal and professional objectives. Finding personal satisfaction and happiness in life is not impossible. If you do not cultivate your own vision for your life, you will ultimately allow other people and circumstances to determine your life's path.

How to Create the Future You Desire for Yourself

It takes time and reflection to properly envision your existence and determine the path you will take through it. In order to put your vision into action, you must not only cultivate vision and perspective, but also employ logic and planning. Your ambitions, desires, and aspirations are the seedlings from which will grow your greatest vision. It will generate energy and enthusiasm and resonate with your values and principles, all of which will strengthen your resolve to explore the possibilities in your life.

What Desires Do You Have?

The query may appear simple at first glance, but the answer is frequently the most difficult. It can be extremely nerve-wracking to grant yourself permission to explore your most private desires. You may also believe that you do not have the time to consider something as preposterous as your life goals; however, it is essential to keep in mind that a life of fulfillment is not typically the result of chance, but rather of deliberate action.

When attempting to determine what you want out of life, it can be beneficial to ask yourself queries that require careful consideration. Consider all aspects of your existence, both the tangible and the intangible, the professional and the personal. Consider your family and friends, your career and success, your health and the quality of your life, your spiritual connection and personal growth, and don't neglect to have fun and enjoy life.

Some suggestions to guide you:

- Always consider why you desire specific items.

- Concentrate on what you do want instead of what you do not want.
- Authorize yourself to indulge in fantasizing.
- Use your creativity. Consider possibilities that you would never have imagined existed.
- Focus on your own objectives rather than those of others.

Some topics to initiate your exploration:

- What do you believe is the most essential aspect of your life? What matters is not what should matter, but what does matter.
- Which aspect of your existence do you believe could be enhanced?
- Put aside the issue of money for a moment; what do you want from your professional life?
- What are some of your most secret desires and passions?
- What are some items that could make your existence happier and more joyful?
- What types of relationships do you desire in your lifetime?

- Which of your current characteristics would you like to develop the most?
- What are a few of your fundamental beliefs? What issues are important to you?
- What abilities do you possess? What distinguishes you from the crowd?
- If you could accomplish anything in the universe, what would you accomplish?
- What sort of legacy do you hope to leave for future generations?

Keeping a journal or constructing a vision board can be very useful for organizing your thoughts if you are a person who appreciates creating things. Include your own inquiries and inquire of others about the life goals they wish to achieve. Take it leisurely and make this workout enjoyable. You may find it useful to set your responses aside for a while and return to them later to see if any of them have changed or if you have anything else to add.

Meditation: Understanding Meditation

In this section, you will learn about Meditation, our relationship with God, the purpose of our lives, the Benefits of Meditation, etc., which will prepare your body and mind for an effective Meditation.

The Inner Quest

Spirituality begins in the truest sense when you ask yourself, "Who am I?" The day you ponder this query, recognize that you have received the Divine call. You may choose to begin the journey immediately or at a later time, but the seed of spirituality has been planted in your consciousness since the day you began contemplating your true origin.

You do not qualify as a Human!

This is the greatest misconception you've held since birth, and it's the cause of all the hardships you've encountered throughout your existence. You are not a human being, but your belief that you are one has made you feel like an ordinary being, limited in your physical abilities, intellect, and ability to connect with the universal forces, etc. You are only concerned with the physical body and believe that you are the physical body!

Who then are You?

You are an angelic being! Yes, that is the truth, the divine reality. Imagine for a moment that you are a part of God or divine forces; your beliefs about yourself, others, and the world as a whole would immediately change, wouldn't they? You are a divine being, a member of the universal forces, and you possess the same qualities and abilities as the larger universal forces!

the capacity to produce

Ability to maintain, mend, and manifest

the power to annihilate

Don't think still? You have the ability to create new corporeal bodies, and your body has the capacity to recover, demolish, and maintain itself, correct?

Before proceeding, you must acknowledge and embrace the fact that you are a divine being inhabiting a human body. You are not the body, you are living in the body, you are traveling in the body, and after some time you will relinquish this body and enter a brand-new body, similar to how you dismantle or sell an old car to acquire a new one. Your entire perspective on yourself and existence has shifted, correct? But this is the truth.

You are a divine being inhabiting a human body and are not a human being.

When you feel apprehensive, encounter fear, anxiety, or are experiencing delusion, repeat to yourself, "I am a divine being currently residing as a human." Yes, that is exactly what you are, and what we are all, Divine!

We have the power to create, the power to cure, and the power to annihilate, and this is what the universe is composed of.

As per Hindu beliefs, there are three powers represented by the three Lords Bramha, Vishnu, and Mahesh. Lord Bramha is the creator, Lord vishnu is the sustainer, and Lord Shiva is the destroyer. According to the Hindu puranas, there are three Shaktis, or energies, represented by three gods.

We are pure energy and nothing but pure energy, and that is what the universe is composed of; the energy in you is the same energy in all other beings, including humans, plants, animals, mountains, rivers, and oceans.

You can neither be made nor annihilated! Only your appearance varies; you are immortal despite having a mortal body. We are all interconnected, one, and members of a larger universal family!

Why do we experience apprehension, concern, and anxiety? Have trust. Lead a fearless, joyful, and tranquil existence. Entrust your life's steering wheel to a higher power and savor the ride. Keep in mind that you are Divine and not human; you are Divine inhabiting a human body.

Do not restrict your potential by considering yourself mortal.

The day you realize you are an immortal and not a mortal marks the beginning of your genuine spiritual voyage. You leave your corporeal remains behind whenever you remove your costume.

When someone states, "I'm just a person," he is truly limiting his ability to accomplish far greater things in life due to his limited perspective. Being human in and of itself is fantastic, and by abandoning the belief that one is an immortal encased in a mortal body and by engaging in certain yogic practices, one can liberate himself from the limitations of the mortal body and perform feats which are far beyond the comprehension of a mortal human mind.

Yes, it is possible to travel at the speed of light in an astral body from one planet to another, and it is also possible to halt the decomposition of the mortal body and be freed from the afflictions and maladies of this world. One can communicate with God, heal others, and create or demolish portions of the natural world.

All of these truths are found in the biographies of Great Yogis and Spiritual Gurus. therefore, what differentiates us from them? They always wanted to live for others, they could control their senses, and they could see beyond the mortal senses' limitations. They utilized the corporeal body to transcend it while still inhabiting it in order to travel far above, deeper, and beyond in order to communicate with the creator and creation. For them, God was a companion, a pure force, and a parent.

They fell in love with God and prayed for the realization of God and the good of the world.

In fact, we are all capable of becoming a true yogi or a Guru; however, in order to do so, we must alter our worldview, work diligently toward God-realization, recognize that we are immortals, and begin living accordingly, without concern for the trivial matters of the mortal senses.

From the Physical to the Subtle

We are such Subtle creatures that we cannot be seen in Physical form by others. Subtle is both our form and our nature. When we begin our descent from the higher worlds to earth, we will assume the form of a subtle body until we merge with the Physical body. Once we inhabit the physical body, we begin to believe that we are that body and begin to neglect our true form and nature, which is the subtle Soul. And when the Physical voyage concludes, the subtle body is liberated and returns to its original location, returning after some time to inhabit a new physical body until one day it decides to remain in his company permanently.

Every entity born on earth is on a never-ending journey from the subtle to the physical and back to the subtle. This voyage is the most difficult for any normal human who believes he is corporeal to comprehend. The only way to comprehend this is through an inward voyage.

Unfortunately, we are only familiar with one or two of the five bodies in which we reside. To comprehend the journey from the Physical to the Subtle, we must comprehend what these five bodies, or Panchakoshas, are.

External Journey

Living with Ego in the belief that I am the Physical body and the agent

The influence of the senses on the body

The senses dictate and determine the types of emotions.

Emotions supplanting Intelligence

The separation of Human Intelligence from the divine entity Soul.

Inner Travel

Understanding that I am not my body

Understanding that I am not my psyche

Closing one's eyelids and directing one's focus inwards

Seeing self as unadulterated energy

Energy-level interaction with the universe

Experiencing and feeling divine joy

God's Relationship with Us

God - Your Employer, Friend, and Parent - what is your true relationship with him?

Try to respond to these inquiries.

1. Do you respect God more than you love him?

2. Do you attempt to bribe him to obtain something from him?

3. Do you truly believe that he will assist you in all circumstances?

4. Are you as relaxed around him as you are with your parents?

Most of us have grown up hearing, "Don't make any mistakes while performing rituals, pujas, etc., or God will punish you!" Take a bath before entering the Puja room or before igniting a Diya, maintain specific postures, and so on.

It is acceptable to observe rituals in certain locations in order to preserve sanctity, but aren't we giving these external practices and beliefs more weight than genuine devotion? Is anxiety not overwhelming the genuine affection and faith we have for God in our daily practices?

How is God able to reprimand his children? Will He, being the embodiment of love, compassion, forgiveness, positivity, and happiness, etc., discipline his offspring for not adhering to certain manmade rituals? Think again!

I believe we must overcome our dread and begin to love him as our genuine parent. Parents demand or anticipate and deserve nothing but love, selfless and unconditional pure affection.

And look at this insane absurdity of life: despite knowing that everything we have is a gift from God, we still attempt to offer him something in exchange for his granting our request. These few examples should prompt us to reconsider and renew our true relationship with God.

Who is the God?

Food for the famished individual
Peace for the disdainful
Assistance for weakened sections
Life on the deathbed for the man
Funding for the economically impoverished
Talent for Ignorance
Understanding for the Ignorant

Wellness for patients
Shelter for destitute

God comes to us in various forms and manners. Let us be thankful for everything we possess.

The design of God and my function.

Everything occurs for a reason, and there is a divine plan behind every event - both good and evil. A seed growing into a massive tree, an infant maturing into a self-aware adult, a river merging with the ocean and then the salty ocean water resurfacing as delicious raindrops - everything is designed, of course by God!

There is a script in everyone's existence, consisting of action, suspense, drama, comedy, and tragedy, similar to a commercial film. Unfortunately, we believe that we are the authors of our own lives; we claim credit for our accomplishments and blame ourselves and others for our transgressions and calamities. God, however, has predetermined our duties, and we are merely acting them out. The moment we realize that we are merely actors playing our respective roles in accordance with God's grander plan, we will be able to concentrate on playing our roles to the best of our abilities rather than constantly praising and criticizing as naïve minuscule beings.

Who authored your FATE?

Certainly not God! What are you saying? I am confident that will be the case your instantaneous response.

Consider for a moment, could God have written such a terrible Fate for you? God and Evil are antonyms, so how could the deity you venerate cause you harm? Does not make sense logically.

The query then becomes, who else has penned your fate? It is you and you alone. Yes, with each passing second, each action, and each thought, you are penning your own Fate and constructing your own future. The day we all realize the significance of this fact, we will likely begin to only consider what is best for everyone, cease harming others, and the world will become a better place.

Start writing a positive future for yourself immediately by thinking well, acting well, and being well.

Life is 10% what occurs and 90% how we respond to it.

The only way we can remain cheerful, tranquil, and collected in all circumstances is by controlling our emotions and acting appropriately in every circumstance. In the end, everything boils down to accepting responsibility for whatever transpires. This ability to remain calm and collected stems from an understanding of the true self and how the laws of nature and the universe operate, as well as how our body, mind, and psyche react to them.

Egoism and Freedom

We use the term EGO every day, but do we truly understand its meaning? In the genuine spiritual sense, EGO denotes "I" (Aham - body manifestation).

E.............Edging
G.............God
O.............Out

This means that when ego arises, we actively push God out of ourselves. In a deeper sense, it means that when we claim credit or hold ourselves accountable for all of our actions, including our achievements, and do not give credit to God, we are edging God out. In reality, everything we do and accomplish in life is the result of God's and nature's bounties, and we are merely tools in the grand scheme of things. Whoever comprehends this will attribute all of his actions to nature and all of his achievements to the divine bounties of God, and will have no "I" - EGO. Once a person begins to recognize that he is, in fact, an Atma (Soul), he feels liberated, begins to see and sense God in everything, attributes everything to God and Nature, and lives in perfect serenity and harmony.

We humans are so ignorant that when we receive something we prayed for, we attempt to corrupt God without realizing that even the bribe was a blessing from him. And when God repeatedly denies our repeated requests, we become angry with him.

When you place me on my knees, I will be in the most effective position to pray!
When you let me down, you literally drive me to God. How often do we pray for divine intervention when we are content and successful? True, very little.

When do we consider God? Yes, after every failure and disgrace at the hands of inhumane individuals.

Don't feel terrible when people deceive you, when you're embarrassed and disappointed. Because each of these occurrences brings you closer to God. When we begin to feel better, however, we make the same error of turning away from God and toward inhuman humans. Therefore, what should be done? Maintain constant contact with God, both in good and bad times, serve as his representative among humans, and strive to remain human among the otherworldly.

When you succeed, praise people for their assistance and cooperation; when you fail, thank those who pushed you closer to God.

Can God make a significant difference in our lives?

This line may be controversial, but you must read it to comprehend my point. Either we exaggerate God's ability to change our lives in the way we desire by attempting to appease him through rituals or bribery, or we neglect our own ability to change our lives for the best and place the responsibility of our lives on God.

Consider the number of times God came to your rescue when you desperately needed him. People assert that absolute faith in God is necessary for His assistance, and they also assert that God is our father. I do not believe any father expects his children to commend, impress, or bribe him to gain his support. Either we have not adequately comprehended God, which is why we engage in such superficial rituals and belief systems, or we have not exerted sufficient effort to determine how we can alter our own future. The concept or fear of God is so deeply ingrained in our minds that we lack sufficient confidence in our own capabilities to accomplish anything without him. One who truly believes in the existence of God will never engage in actions that are not sanctioned by him.

I believe that we have been sufficiently indoctrinated since infancy to believe in a certain form of godliness, and we do not venture to question whether this is correct or not. I do not doubt the existence of God; there must be someone seated somewhere overseeing the universe's daily affairs. I am only pondering the form in which we know him; I am querying the manner in which we are led to believe that God, if delighted, will rectify our lives regardless of our past actions.

Experience has taught me that I should focus more on my karmas (actions) and have faith in my own abilities, rather than relying on God's pleasure with rituals to alter my future. I have learned that I should take responsibility for my past, present, and future rather than putting it on God's shoulders.

Existence of God's dilemma!

If there is a God, He should assist all of his offspring who are in need. But is he assisting? No ! What does this signifier? Does this imply that there is no God or that He exists but does not assist His children? because He wants the law of Karma (what you produce is what you reap) to determine His children's destinies and He does not wish to intervene?

If He wants His children's destinies to be determined by Karmas and does not wish to interfere with its operations, then why would anyone seek His assistance?

It has been said that when in difficulty, one should seek God's assistance, and if one has faith, God will indeed assist. However, the same God in the Gita stated that actions have consequences (present Karmas will determine the future). However, Krishna also says in the Gita that whoever approaches Him will always receive His favors.

Then, does God contradict Himself, or are we incapable of understanding the truth? Today, people are warring and murdering in God's name. Millions of people perform pujas and travel tens of thousands of kilometers to get a glimpse of their god at religious sites. But has anyone ever seen God? No! At most, some may have sensed His existence, but no one has seen Him!

Will the enigma of God's existence remain unresolved forever, or will we all be enlightened one day? Currently, it remains a simple query.

Instead of following God, follow the Godliness of that God.

When it comes to the worship of a particular God, we all have our own choices and preferences, for reasons that are difficult to comprehend. That's acceptable, since we live in a democracy where freedom of religion is guaranteed by our constitution.

But the irony is that we worship only the physical structure (statue, photograph, etc.) of the God, but we don't bother to follow the Godliness of that particular God, meaning we don't live by the teachings or principles of that God, for example, Lord Krishna's followers should be living according to the Gita, Lord Rama's devotees should never lie, should never look at other women, etc. However, we claim and proclaim ourselves to be the confident adherents or devotees of that particular God, despite not adhering to that God's actual teachings.

Either we do not know or have forgotten the reason for following a particular

God, or our parents forced us as children to venerate a particular God without explaining the reason.

It is regrettable that the majority of us as parents tell our children that God's blessings will determine their future rather than their own virtues, efforts, and attitude. Fear and insecurity motivate the concept of God more than faith, according to research.

When one takes a closer look, the world resembles a collection of bewildered, fearful, and self-centered individuals who pray and beseech the god of their choice for either material or spiritual gain without bothering to Know, comprehend, and live by the doctrines and principles of that particular god.

In one sentence, we all want something from our God, but we're not concerned with understanding and obeying that God's divinity!

When God created the universe, He imbued it with divine qualities such as happiness, serenity, wisdom, gratitude, and compassion, then encased them in a priceless treasure. He then created humanity with the desire that every human possess these divine attributes. God, however, wanted us to exert effort and acquire these divinities; He did not want to give them to us for nothing. Therefore, He has created a seal and a key for this treasure. Then, he continued to ponder where to conceal this key. First, he considered hiding it in some deep caves in the Himalayas, but then he realized that man would eventually reach there. Next, he considered burying it in the depths of the ocean, but felt that man would eventually reach there as well in his quest for the treasure. He continued to consider every possible place where man could not easily reach it, until he realized that there is only one place where man would not search: within himself. Therefore, the key to unlocking the divine treasure resides within us, not in a temple or ashram. And the only way to get there is through an introspective procedure - meditation.

Through the techniques of profound meditation, we can discover the key to the divine treasure, which contains an abundance of happiness, pleasure, divine knowledge, ecstasy, etc.

However, reaching deep within ourselves is more challenging than space exploration, deep-sea diving, or any other activity you can imagine. To enter this world, you must first demolish the EGO wall that has been constructed around you and control your senses to obtain a passport. It requires a great deal of concentration, altruistic thought and action, a genuine comprehension of the self and our relationship with God, just to board the plane that can take us deep within ourselves.

However, despite the difficulty, we should not abandon faith of achieving our objective. The ultimate purpose of our lives should be to one day locate the key and release the treasure. Devote a few minutes per day to traveling within yourself, realizing yourself, sensing the divinity within you, and releasing yourself from the senses and worldly attachments. To get closer to this key, conduct an introspective exploration. Keeping the body healthy, the mind optimistic, and engaging in soulful behavior will earn you the Key and make your journey easier.

God created Humans to realize God!

It is written and believed that even after creating millions of different species of living beings, God was not satisfied because none of his creations were able to comprehend Him!

And as a result, God created human beings, endowed them with the capacity to reason, the capacity to comprehend God's existence and the capacity to recognize God, and it was only with the creation of human beings that God was ultimately satiated.

Today, however, the same individual has neglected his creator and, more significantly, the purpose of his creation, which is to realize the creator (God).

Everyone is in a frantic dash to satiate his senses, believing it to be the pinnacle of pleasure, but in reality, he is a slave to his senses and a prisoner to his body.

To realize genuine pleasure, he must ponder beyond the body and realize the true existence and the existence's creator. The purpose of a human existence is incomplete and meaningless if God is not realized.

The only difference between humans and other animals is that humans can pursue and realize God, whereas living a life without doing so or at least attempting to do so is equivalent to that of an animal. Therefore, devote a small amount of time each day to drawing closer to God, as that is our primary purpose as humans.

Let's call HIM occasionally.

We live in an age of advanced communication, and communication instruments have vastly improved over the past two or three decades. But we have not yet invented a communication instrument, device, or mechanism for communicating directly with HIM. We frequently call our friends, family, customers, clients, etc. for various reasons. However, how often do we dial HIS number to say "Thank you" for human life?

Let's dial HIM once in a while to share our success stories, Let's dial HIM once in a while to get essential life advice, and let's dial HIM once in a while to say "Everything is fine in our life" because of HIS blessings.

HIS phone will never be active for us, and HE will never disconnect our call. In fact, HE will be just as interested in listening to and conversing with us as we are. The difficulty is locating HIS contact number so that HE can be reached. The obstacle is to invent or discover a compatible handset device. However, Let's keep dialing HIM through whatever device we are currently using, Let's keep dialing HIS number, whichever one we believe to be HIS, as we never know when we will strike HIS number, nor when HE will answer our call and greet us. So, let's continue to call HIM on occasion.

Some say that because HE is available everywhere, HE can be contacted at any time and that HE is constantly watching and listening to us. Some suggest Meditation as a powerful method for establishing contact with HIM, while others assert that nothing but unadulterated devotion is sufficient, and still others assert that our KARMA is the most important factor for communicating with HIM. Perhaps they are all correct, so let's test all of them if necessary. But let's call HIM to let HIM know that we've realized that we are HIS offspring and that we need HIS help to live by HIS principles on this planet during these challenging times in order to remain pure, devout, honest, optimistic, and joyful. Let's continue dialing HIM until we are able to communicate with HIM and ask HIM to bless us with true self-realization and eternal pleasure. Let's not give up! Let's continue dialing HIM until HE answers.

This is a brief supplication.

I was ignorant then, and I continue to be naive now.
Bless me with the insight to entirely surrender to you, to have absolute faith in you without fear or doubt, and to be in eternal love with you.
Bless me with the understanding that contentment is found in letting go, not in acquiring more.

Bless me with the understanding that love consists of offering it to others rather than pursuing it from them.

Bless me with the understanding that happiness, serenity, and tranquility are not found in the future or the past, but rather in the present.

Bestow upon me eternal pleasure and wisdom, Paramatma.

The First Exercise Is Breathing Through The Spine

The First exercise is one of the most fundamental, and many spiritual individuals perform it daily. Before I describe the techniques, you should be aware that these exercises rely heavily on your respiration. Important to meditation is the use of respiration, and both exercises are types of meditation or yoga techniques. This strategy is also known as inhaling through the vertebrae. While breathing through the vertebrae, you will transfer the sexual energy (Chi energy in Chinese) up towards the brain and down into the solar plexus chakra from the root Chakra. It is crucial to transfer the energy back down to another power center in the body because other areas, including the head and other chakras associated with body parts, cannot manage the energy, resulting in severe migraines or kundalini-like symptoms.

If you are new to the realm of meditation, I recommend that you simply follow the fundamental instructions.

Do not attempt this if you are expectant, have severe spine-related issues, or are experiencing unbearable agony elsewhere.

Step one: Sit with your legs crossed or on a chair with your feet level on the ground and your knees bent to 90 degrees with your back erect. You can perform this action while seated on any surface.

Step two: clench your genital muscles, draw your midsection in, and take a deep breath. Your tongue should be reaching the bottom of your mouth, and your jawline should be as near to your torso as possible without causing pain. Additionally, your spine should be slightly arched.

While exhaling, erect your back, expand your torso, and raise your jaw.

Step four: Relax your genital muscles and begin to exhale slowly. As you exhale, curve your back down as if you were bowing, but do not bend over. While exhaling entirely, press your tongue against the roof of your mouth and stretch your stomach out.

DO THIS NINE TIMES. At least twice daily, nine times upon awakening and nine times upon retiring.

On the fourth day, individuals between the ages of 19 and 30 will experience an increase in sexual energy. Rather than dissipate this energy through masturbation, simply increase your physical activity and you should be alright. THE SECOND EXERCISE SHOULD BE ADDED TO THE PROGRAM IF YOU STILL FEEL A STRONG NEED TO BUILD SEXUAL ENERGY.

Every eighth or ninth day, individuals aged 29 to 50 will experience a surge in sexual energy.

I would advise against ejaculating during this time. You will have the opportunity to advance to the next level of spiritual development every fourth day, resulting in increased vitality and strength within the body. More seminal fluid will help nourish the body, particularly if you engage in frequent masturbation or frequent sexual activity with a partner.

Benefits Of Meditation

The benefits of meditation for business proprietors and entrepreneurs

If you've attempted to start a business, you're familiar with the tension that comes with long hours of work, overcoming unanticipated obstacles, and assuming greater responsibilities. You find it challenging to consume well and even more challenging to sleep well. Consequently, making time for meditation seems unattainable.

Daily, you encounter unavoidable and natural tension. However, if you continue to let tension build up, it can be detrimental to your mind and body. It can result in a variety of health problems, including hypertension, digestive issues, gastric disturbances, indigestion, chest symptoms, and difficulty resting.

The accumulation of tension can exacerbate disease symptoms and delay the healing of ailments and injuries.

The benefits of meditation for business proprietors and entrepreneurs are numerous. By routinely meditating, you can calm your body and psyche. Meditation's calming effect can relieve the body of tension.

If a task necessitates problem-solving and innovative inputs, you must focus intently on it. With meditation, you can handle any information that arises throughout the day.

Considering the mental and physical advantages of incorporating meditation into a healthy lifestyle, it is simple to see why so many business owners are turning to it. By taking some time to recharge and unwind through meditation, you can increase your effectiveness and productivity for the day, allowing you to complete more tasks.

After completing a daily meditation session, you can attain a newfound state of mindfulness. This state can transform mundane activities such as commuting, working, filing documents, or preparing a cup of coffee into a form of meditative concentration.

Increasing employee morale through meditation in the workplace

Some corporations employ the services of meditation specialists to encourage their employees. This will require employees to participate in group meditation sessions. Meditation has three benefits for corporations.

It maintains the employees' health and wellness.

It contributes to enhanced employee productivity.

It enhances worker morale.

When employees meditate on a regular basis, business proprietors can reduce absenteeism costs. This is because meditation has health benefits. The employees' bodies will remain healthy, resulting in fewer employees calling in unwell. Employers' assistance will foster a sense of affinity among the workforce.

This will result in increased overall job satisfaction.

Regular meditation can increase productivity, particularly for those whose jobs require them to make creative contributions or maintain focus for extended periods of time. Included in this category are architects, programmers, engineers, and artists.

Employees' capacity to learn can be enhanced through meditation because it improves memory retention. When an employee is able to keep his or her mind clear of distractions, he or she is able to concentrate on the task at hand and increase productivity.

Meditation can enhance employee morale for a variety of reasons. Due to shared experiences, employees develop emotional closeness through group meditation. As a result of lowering their emotional defenses, meditation can facilitate effective teamwork on group initiatives. This will result in greater support for one another when deadlines, demands, or job specifications are altered.

Employees develop a sense that their employers care about their well-being as a result of their employers' suggestion of group meditation as a means of boosting productivity and enhancing health. Companies that take pride in their employees inspire employee loyalty.

What Companions Want

There is only one factor that genuinely attracts a partner. It transcends class, nationality, religion, and every other status. People can acquire or be born with wealth, notoriety, and power, among other attributes, to attract companions. In this volume, however, I will examine the spiritual aspect and search within for the answers. And there is one trait that transcends all of these physical characteristics and makes all people attractive. That quality is self-assurance. A throng of 20,000 people can be hypnotized for hours by a person's charismatic appeal and unwavering self-assurance.

The difficulty is that you cannot feign confidence. Moreover, we are not taught how to obtain it. We simply know we desire it. And if we already possess it, we desire even more of it. This is where mindfulness is most useful in this situation. We are apathetic, heedless of our surroundings, and disconnected from others when we lack confidence.

You cannot simply tell yourself, "Be confident," and expect it to be effective. If it were that simple, everyone would be Mick Jagger. Some individuals may be born with it. Mindfulness can help the rest of us attain a genuine, genuine, profound, impregnable confidence. It accomplishes this by inculcating the habit of being present and free of thought.

With mindfulness, there are no negative notions, such as "I don't know," that can enter the mind prior to a public speech. Should I proceed? Perhaps I shouldn't? What will occur? All of this could go terribly awry." This is because you are only fixated on the present moment, in which you only need to take one more step, then another. There is no "What will happen in an hour if my speech is subpar?" Nor will you wonder, "What will happen if I go speak to that lad or girl? What if they disapprove of me?"

The current instant is devoid of dread. There are no inactions. Fear exists only in the mind when we fret about the future, dwell on misgivings from the past, or recall traumatic memories. Presently, however, everything is as it should be. When we are truly present, we use our senses with greater sensitivity. We are utilizing our focus and attention to simply observe and respond to whatever is occurring. In the present moment, there is no dread of the future, no anxiety over what may occur, no regret for the past, and no fixation or obsession with a desired outcome. There is only tranquility and serenity because you know you can handle whatever comes your way with greater clarity and sagacity. If you continue to do your best in the present, you will eventually have a fulfilling existence.

Anyone who possesses innate confidence intuitively understands the power of presence. They are entirely present in conversations, listen attentively without considering what they will say next, and respond spontaneously. They simply allow the energy transfer that occurs between two individuals during a conversation, similar to a volleyball of energy being passed back and forth. Attractive is their attention and focus on others without self-obsession or doubt. This level of unadulterated assurance can only be attained through mindfulness.

Some individuals have a greater proclivity than others to be overly introverted. They may experience increased anxiety and concern in social situations. With mindfulness and presence, it is impossible to be anxious about the future or how something could go awry. There is only confidence and the knowledge that everything will be alright and that you can survive any situation without difficulty.

With mindfulness, skepticism has no place in the mind. In fact, doubt and insecurity are indicators of a low sense of self-worth and image. The image of high self-worth projected by confidence is inherently attractive. Therefore, there are a variety of materialistic things we can do to make ourselves more alluring in order to attract the ideal partner. But even these qualities pale in comparison to confidence. Due to their confidence, poor and even less-than-averagely attractive individuals have been able to date supermodels. I will demonstrate how you, too, can achieve this self-assurance.

Principal Advantages Of Mindful Breathing

All vital processes involve oxidation and reduction: without oxygen, there is no life. Our cells obtain their oxygen supply from blood. As oxygen-deficient blood circulates through our arteries, the vitality of each cell is diminished.

If you learn to breathe correctly, the benefits are substantial: the body becomes rigid and healthy, the surplus fat dissipates, the face emanates, the eyes glitter, and the entire personality exudes a special appeal. Additionally, the voice becomes pleasant and musical. A person who has mastered the art of respiration is no longer an accessible target for disease. After a lengthy trek in the great outdoors, it is important to recollect your appetite. The purification of the entire body facilitates awareness and appropriate action.

Advantages of Mindful Breathing

Mindful breathing has the ability to harmonize the body, mind, spirit, and emotions. The advantages of each aircraft are as follows:

In physical terms

You feel more calm and spontaneous, your vitality increases, your energy and emotions renew, and your metabolic functions improve.

To relieve suffering

Breathing deeply can help alleviate pain naturally. In a recent study involving 14 patients with fibromyalgia (a disease characterized by chronic pain), researchers determined that yoga, meditation, and deep breathing had a very favorable impact on the intervention group's fibromyalgia symptoms, including pain alleviation.[1].

On an emotional level, Mindful Breathing enhances self-confidence and mends relationships with others; you lose emotional burdens and gain insight into your personal history and why you have certain personality traits. You learn to forgive yourself, other people, and life itself. You are less influenced by your emotions, and you connect independently with the environment.

Reduces tension

Stress is common, essential, and not always negative. There is beneficial tension (such as having an infant) and severe anxiety (such as being dismissed from a job). Unfortunately, our bodies are incapable of distinguishing between them. Stress contributes to a broad range of health issues, so it is essential to reduce and manage it. Deep respiration induces relaxation and slumber in the body.

Think Straight

In a 2007 study, several students participated in meditation and Mindful Breathing in the hopes that stress reduction would improve their academic performance. The researchers concluded that "the students reduced their level of exam anxiety, nervousness, and lack of self-confidence, and improved their ability to concentrate" [2].

Sleep better

People who are exposed to chronic tension are more likely to develop insomnia. These individuals have elevated levels of the stress hormone cortisol. When cortisol is released in the body, sleep becomes extremely difficult because the body has a harder time relaxing.

Mindful Breathing promotes relaxation and consequently effects the parasympathetic nervous system, thereby interrupting the cycle of insomnia.

On a mental level, it is cognizant of the constraints we face. Improve the ability to observe oneself objectively. Enhance your creativity and make you more intuitive. Assist in generating intelligent concepts to take command of your life and initiatives. Enhance your ability to observe and address your requirements.

You live transpersonal and fulfillment experiences on a spiritual level. The strengthening of the SELF reduces the dread of existing, having emotions, and being able to express them. Discover new capacities for loving and being loved. Gleichzeitig enables us to connect with spaces and spiritual states in order to observe our mind through them.

Practice

Feel the air flowing into and out of your nostril as you inhale and exhale. Initially, your respiration may not be relaxed. However, after practicing Mindful Breathing for a while, you will notice that it becomes lighter, more natural, and increasingly tranquil. You can return to this tranquil source of vitality whenever you are walking, gardening, typing, or performing any other activity.

You can tell yourself, "Breathing, I am aware that I am inhaling."

Exhale, I am certain I exhale.

You may wish to abbreviate this after a few breaths to "inside, outside." While your focus is on inhaling and exhaling, your intellect ceases to function. Now, your mind has an opportunity to relax. In our daily lives, we believe excessively.

It is fantastic to give your mind an opportunity to cease pondering.

What does breathe mean, given that I am inhaling?

I am aware that I breathe without any thought. You breathe in and out merely to be aware that something is occurring. When you inhale and concentrate on your breath, you reconnect your consciousness with your body. Breathing alone can assist in returning the consciousness to the body. When the mind and body unite, you can inhabit the present moment in its entirety.

"Breathe, I know I'm breathing" is a synonym for "breathe in, I feel alive." Life is within you and all around you, life with all its marvels: the sun, the blue sky, and the autumn foliage. To connect with the healing elements, rejuvenation, and sustenance of the life that is within and around you, it is essential to visit the present moment's domicile. A gentle smile can relax all the facial muscles.

I inhale and recognize the sky as blue.

I exhale and smile while gazing at the blue sky.

As I inhale, I am aware of the gorgeous autumn foliage.

I exhale and beam as I observe the gorgeous autumn foliage.

This can be shortened to 'blue sky' by inhaling and 'smile' by exhaling. Then, 'falling foliage' to inspire and 'laugh' to breathe. When you practice breathing in this manner, you encounter all of life's marvels. Life's splendor nourishes you. You are liberated from your anxieties and concerns. You become acquainted with your respiration and physique. Your physique is excellent. Your eyes are lovely; if you open them, you can touch a paradise of shapes and hues. Your hearing are remarkable. Your hearing allow you to hear a variety of sounds, including music, a bird's melody, and the breeze flowing through the pine trees. When you focus on your inhalation and exhalation, you return to the present moment, the here and now, and you experience existence.

I inhale and observe my respiration as I travel.

As I exhale, I continue to exhale throughout the trip.

Initially, you may experience somewhat labored or unusual respiration. Your respiration is influenced by your body and emotions. Your respiration will be affected if your body is in tension or pain, or if you are experiencing excruciating sensations. Observe your respiration and engage in Mindful respiration.

I am aware that I am inhaling in.

Exhale, I am certain I exhale.

I chuckle at my own exhalation.

Exhaling, I chuckle at my exhalation.

Never compel yourself to breathe. If your respiration is shallow, it should be rapid. If it's not very silent, let it be. Simply observe, and your respiration quality will gradually improve over time. Full awareness of the breath identifies and cherishes your inhalation and exhalation like a mother holding her infant in her arms as she welcomes him home. You will be astonished at how quickly your respiration improves after one or two minutes. Your respiration grows deeper. Your exhalation will slow down. Your respiration becomes more harmonious and relaxed.

I observe that my inspiration deepens as I breathe.

I observe that my exhalation decreases as I exhale.

You can bring peace, serenity, and harmony to your body when you observe that your inhalation and exhalation have become calmer, deeper, and slower. This is your opportunity to acknowledge your body's existence and make friends with it.

I am conscious of my body as I breathe.

I discharge all tension in my body as I exhale.

These respiration exercises originated with the Buddha. They are as straightforward as a child's pastime. Put your hand on your midriff if it helps. When you breathe in, your stomach will rise, and when you breathe out, your stomach will fall. Up down. Particularly when lying down, it is easy to sense your midsection rise and fall. You are conscious of your entire inhalation and exhalation. You enjoy exhaling in this fashion. You no longer contemplate the past, future, your endeavors, or your suffering. The act of respiration becomes pleasurable, a reminder of life itself.

I take pleasure in my inhalation.

I appreciate my exhalation

Later, when you are able to provide your body with peace and harmony and assist it in releasing tension, you will be able to identify and recognize your feelings and emotions.

I am conscious of the agonizing emotions within me as I inhale.

I exhale and smile at the agonizing sensation within me.

There is both an excruciating sensation and a complete awareness. All knowledge is like a mother caressing the senses with tenderness. Full awareness is always the total awareness of something. When you breathe with complete awareness, you have complete respiratory awareness. If you walk with complete awareness, you will experience the full sensation of strolling. If you imbibe with complete awareness, you are imbibing with complete awareness. If you are aware of your emotions, you have a complete understanding of them. It is possible to intervene with complete knowledge in any physical or mental event, bringing about recognition and illumination.

Below, I will leave you with a poem to practice, recite it occasionally while you smile and breathe:

I am aware that I am inhaling in.

Exhale, I am certain I exhale.

As I inhale more deeply, I exhale more slowly.

Breathing As I exhale, I calm my body and feel at peace.

I smile as I exhale and let go while breathing.

I am aware that the present moment is a beautiful one.

This can be shortened by breathing out a word or phrase.

In out.

Deep, sluggish

Calm, comfortable.

I giggle, therefore I am liberated.

Present moment, gorgeous moment.

The only moment that is real is the present moment. Your primary responsibility is to be in the present moment and to appreciate it.

Managing Unsettling Emotions

When we begin meditating for the first time, we are likely to experience a range of emotions, some of which may be positive, others negative, and still others impartial. During meditation, we may experience a disagreeable emotion that we would rather avoid than dwell with. In this instance, however, the meditation instruction is to remind yourself that this is merely a sensation; in doing so, you will feel less disturbed. Obviously, you are not attempting to befriend the disagreeable emotion, but rather to adopt a neutral stance towards it. Interestingly, the instruction remains the same if we experience ecstatic joy during meditation. Even though these feelings may be a sign of progress, we should recognize that they are temporary and approach them with a neutral attitude, without becoming overly enthusiastic about the situation and especially without becoming attached to feelings of happiness. There is nothing wrong with feeling fantastic, and it is problematic to attempt to suppress these sentiments. Nonetheless, we should not adhere to this form of emotion. Essentially, the instruction is to remain calm and continue moving forward regardless of what occurs. This is how we arrive at enlightenment.

Where do meditative disturbances originate from? So many meditative obstacles exist, and they take so many forms. According to Buddhist texts, familiarity with negative mental states such as ignorance, attachment, and aversion causes meditation disturbances. In meditation, mental wandering occurs, for instance, due to attachment to numerous physically pleasurable objects. Regret is another prevalent emotion that disturbs people's meditation. During meditation, you may wonder, "Did I do the right thing or the wrong thing?" These thoughts occupy your consciousness and distract you from the object of your meditation. It is healthy to feel regret for your negative actions, but you should not allow regret or resentment to interfere with your concentration or impair your meditation practice. When you begin to experience regret or resentment, avoid thinking about the object that is causing these emotions. You must shift your attention to something else, such as something attractive. There is a time for regretting counterproductive actions, but that time is not during meditation. The mind devises a variety of creative escape routes from meditation.

Another prevalent meditation issue is lethargy. Sluggishness is characterized by a weighty feeling in the body and psyche. It indicates that you are unable to concentrate with a sharp mind. Sleepiness is comparable. If you are feeling lethargic, you should visualize something extremely joyous and full of delight so that it enlivens and rouses you. If you are feeling drowsy while attempting to meditate, avoid closing your eyes. When you open your eyes, it is more likely that you will remain alert. Thus, this is one method to combat lethargy.

Perhaps the greatest obstacle of all is uncertainty. Regarding some aspect of the truth, doubt is having two minds. If we have doubts regarding the benefits of meditation, we will lack the motivation to practice. It is therefore essential that whenever you have even the slightest doubt, you consult your teacher or someone else who is qualified to solve your problem and dispel your uncertainty. Asking someone who has more doubts than you would only add to your confusion. When you have doubt, you will feel as though an alien is moving inside of you. But once you have resolved your uncertainties, you will feel very at ease.

Want and malice are two additional significant obstacles to meditation. The only result of craving is dissatisfaction, which will interfere with your meditation. Malice is a form of agitation that manifests as a desire to harm others. However, this emotion is not only detrimental to others, but to ourselves as well. It is a very destructive and upsetting emotion that destroys our mental serenity and tranquility. When such negative energy arises, one should engage in acts of compassion and affection. Once you have subdued all of these impediments and dealt with them as soon as they appear, your meditation will commence.

It is essential to care for and nurture yourself, particularly by averting these detrimental emotions. We should address our emotions instead of ignoring them. You want to meditate in order to cultivate serenity, so it should not become a source of additional problems. Sometimes, we sustain ourselves with our wrath, envy, and other toxins, which is detrimental to our mental and physical health. Therefore, we must be wise enough to refrain from feeding our wrath. Please exercise forbearance, as it is the most important virtue to cultivate. In Buddhism, you are considered a great practitioner not based on the number of hours you have meditated or mantras you have recited, but on the basis of your behavior, which reflects your interior beliefs.

There is a very skillful method to cope with negative emotions: when we become aware of a negative emotion, we refrain from giving it our attention. When driving on the side of the road, for instance, we pass many different people, objects, and advertising signs, but we should always keep our attention on the road. Otherwise we will get into a catastrophe. Meditation is comparable. Naturally, a variety of distracting thoughts and emotions will arise, but if you do not pursue them, you will observe that they disappear on their own. They do not require your accompaniment!

People frequently inquire about the Vajrayna technique for managing negative emotions. However, both Strayna and Vajrayna gaze directly at the emotion itself. Therefore, a person who desires to practice Vajrayna must also comprehend Strayna and specifically Mahyna techniques. Examining animosity itself is one method for purifying oneself. Other methods exist; they may appear extreme to those who only practice Strayna, but they are extremely effective. As an analogy, when we get water in our ear, we shake our head or use a cotton swab to eliminate the water. There is a second method that involves pouring more water into the ear to remove all the water. When one's finger is scorched, it is natural to wash it under cool water to alleviate the discomfort. However, there is a method that involves shaking the charred finger near a fire, which is said to alleviate the agony. These analogies illustrate how the Vajrayna method for coping with negative emotions is a transformation of our view of the world from ordinary to extraordinary, although I have never attempted them. For instance, despite the fact that wrathful deities appear ferocious and furious, they are actually manifestations of compassion. To correctly comprehend Vajrayna practice, one must receive instruction from a genuine guru.

As practitioners, we must comprehend our minds and our psychology, as well as the specific conditions that foster positive mental qualities. For instance, we should be aware of how much slumber we require. Sleep nourishes the psyche and body. There are certainly excellent masters who do not require much sleep and can meditate throughout the day. However, the majority of individuals require adequate slumber. If we are able to meditate all day without much sleep but then become irritable, it is pointless. Our objective is to eliminate negative emotions and cultivate positive ones, not to be able to meditate nonstop. We cannot compel our bodies to exceed their limits. Otherwise, more problems will ensue. Prioritize quality over quantity by meditating daily for lesser durations. In this manner, we can progressively develop a consistent practice.

www.ingramcontent.com/pod-product-compliance
Lightning Source LLC
Chambersburg PA
CBHW050244120526
44590CB00016B/2213